Are We Home Yet?

Are We Home Yet?

By

Mark H. Glissmeyer

Gradina Books

ISBN-13: 978-0-9985416-8-6

Introduction:

This book begins in a car,
on a trip that seems real far,
with a dad who's driving home,
in the backseat is young Jerome.

Are we home yet?

Yes, we're almost there,
but don't get out of your chair.

When are we there?

When we get there.
Now stay in your chair.

Are we home yet?

Yes, we're almost there.
Now stop pulling my hair.

When are we getting there?

Would you stop it, I swear.
We're almost nearly there.

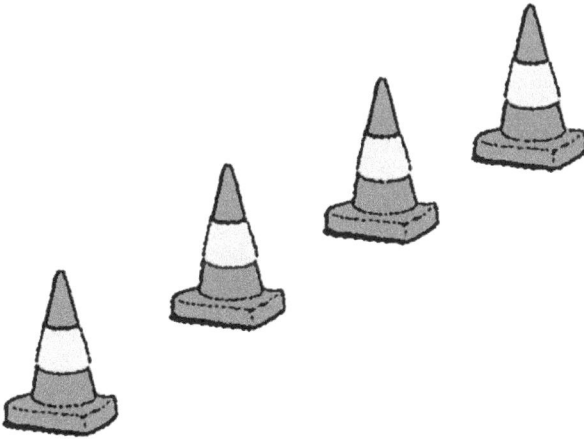

Is that it there?

It's somewhere over there.
Now stop it now, I swear.

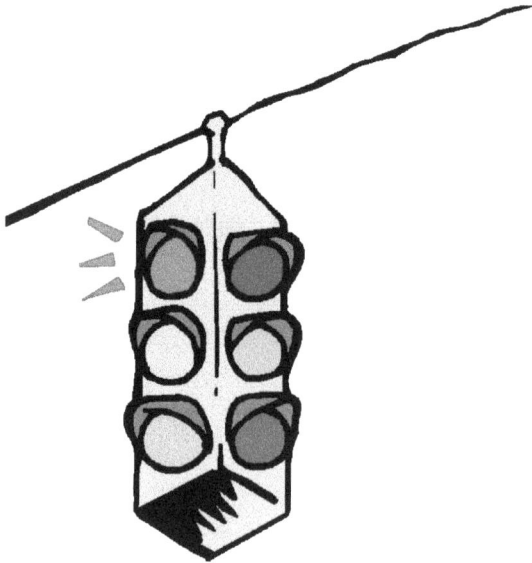

Are we ever gonna get there?

We'll make it home, I swear.
It's somewhere over there.

When do we get there?

It's a little ways over there.
Now stay seated in that chair.

Is that it over there?

You'll see it soon, I swear.
Now stop pulling my hair.

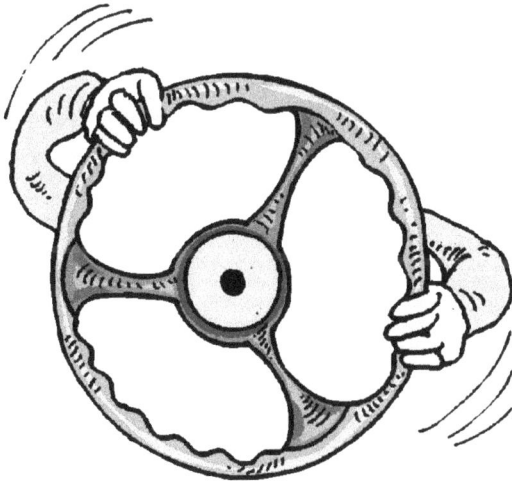

This doesn't seem fair.

Nothing in life is fair.
Now stay seated in that chair.

Are we almost getting there?

Yes, we're almost nearly there.
Now pretend you just don't care.

How come we aren't there?

We'll make it there, I swear.
Now stop pushing my chair.

This is so unfair.

We'll get there soon, I swear.
Now sit back in your chair.

DO
NOT
PASS

How much longer to get there?

Now we're almost there.
It's just over there.

Is that it over there?

Stop pushing my chair.
I told you it's over there.

Why can't we get there?

We'll get there soon, I swear.
It's right over there.

When are we there?

We're passing by a thoroughfare.
It's right beyond there.

Is that it over there?

I think I need some air.
Now stay seated in that chair.

How much longer to get there?

Keep watching over there.
Only a little longer, I swear.

Can we please get there?

I wish we're already there.
Now stop grabbing my hair.

Are you sure we're almost there?

I said we're almost there.
Now sit back and stay in that chair.

Is that it over there?

Just watch way over there.
It's just a little longer, I swear.

I think I see it right there.

It's getting closer, I swear.
Just keep watching over there.

I think I peed my chair.

Just hold it in, I swear.
Now we're almost there.

How much longer there?

We're almost home, I swear.
Just sit back in your chair.

Is that it over there?

It's just past the corner there,
so don't hit my chair.

How much longer there?

I swear it's over there.
We'll follow that clunker there.

Oh crap, is that it there?

Don't you ever swear!
And stop pulling my hair.

Shouldn't we already be there?

Just a minute more in your chair.
That's our house right there.

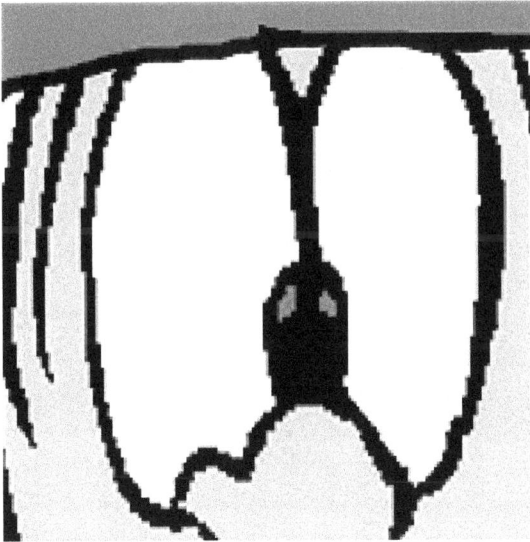

That's the right street there?

We're pulling up now, I swear.
Just a minute more in that chair!

WE'RE THERE!
WE'RE THERE!
WE'RE THERE!

That was the worst trip, I swear.
Now let's get you out of there!

The End???????

No, now on to the next chapter.

What's on TV.

Daddy, what's on TV?

It's on now so let's see.
I think that's channel three.

That's not what I want to see.

I'm taking my vitamin E.
Just wait there for me.

Are you sure it's channel three?

I'm also making some tea.
Just wait there and see.

Are you going to drink that with me?

It's only some herbal tea.
Just wait there, you'll see.

I don't like channel three.

It's commercials on now, you'll see.
Just wait there for me.

I want some herbal tea.

Just sit and wait for me.
I'm almost there, you'll see.

Now I have to pee.

Just sit and wait for me,
I'll change it from channel three.

Is this free TV?

No, we have to pay a fee.
Now sit and wait for me.

Can I help you make that tea?

No, just sit and wait for me.
You wanted to watch TV.

I don't like channel three.

The commercials are over, you'll see.
Now sit and wait for me.

How much do we pay to see?

Don't worry about that fee.
Just sit and wait for me.

The commercials are still on three.

They'll be over soon, you'll see.
Now stop asking me.

I really have to pee.

Can I please make my tea?
Just watch and wait for me.

The End???????

No, now on to the next chapter.

Get your butt in bed.

But I 'm not ready for bed.

Listen to what I said,
now it's time for bed.

I want a piece of bread.

You can't have any bread.
Now get your butt to bed.

What about that book you read?

It's laying under your bed.
Now please do what I said.

Just one small piece of bread?

You can't have any bread.
Now get your butt in bed.

That's not what mommy said.

It's too late to give you bread.
Now listen to what I said.

I want that book you read.

It was under your little bed.
Now try and sleep instead.

Do I have to go to bed?

That's already what I said.
Now get your butt to bed.

I'm still hungry for some bread.

But you've already been fed.
Now get your butt in bed.

Mommy said it's cornbread.

It's too late for cornbread.
Now go to sleep instead.

When can I play with Ted?

Tonight you'll sleep instead.
Now get your butt in bed.

Daddy, I want to go to bed.

"HURRAY, HURRAY," daddy said,
and he placed Jerome in his bed.

So Jerome nods off and dreams.
And everything's right, it seems.

Finally, the End.
Signed, a tired Daddy

Lightning Source UK Ltd.
Milton Keynes UK
UKHW011537071221
395215UK00002B/84